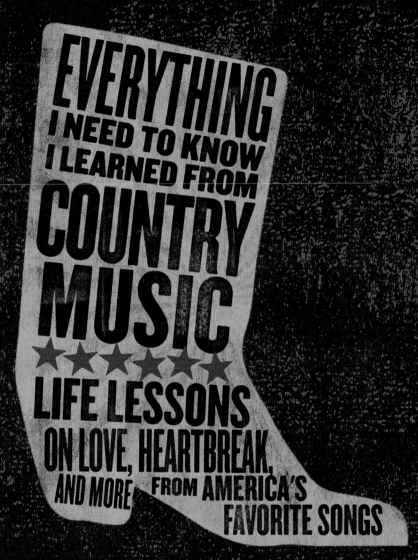

EVERYTHING
I NEED TO KNOW
I LEARNED FROM
COUNTRY
MUSIC

★★★★★

LIFE LESSONS
ON LOVE, HEARTBREAK, AND MORE FROM AMERICA'S FAVORITE SONGS

STELLA BARNES · ILLUSTRATED BY **BOB DELEVANTE**

CASTLE POINT BOOKS
NEW YORK

Everything I Need to Know I Learned from Country Music

Copyright © 2022 by St. Martin's Press.

All rights reserved. Printed in China.

For information, address St. Martin's Publishing Group,

120 Broadway, New York, NY 10271.

www.castlepointbooks.com

The Castle Point Books trademark is owned by Castle Point Publishing, LLC.

Castle Point books are published and distributed by St. Martin's Publishing Group.

ISBN 978-1-250-28354-2 (trade paperback)

ISBN 978-1-250-28386-3 [ebook]

Design by Katie Jennings Campbell

Edited by Jennifer Calvert

Our books may be purchased in bulk for promotional, educational, or business use.

Please contact your local bookseller or the Macmillan Corporate and Premium Sales

Department at 1-800-221-7945, extension 5442, or by email at

MacmillanSpecialMarkets@macmillan.com.

First Edition: 2022

10 9 8 7 6 5 4 3 2 1

"COUNTRY MUSIC
isn't a **GUITAR**, it isn't a **BANJO**,
it isn't a **MELODY**, it isn't a **LYRIC**.
IT'S A FEELING."

—WAYLON JENNINGS

CONTENTS

SONGS FOR THE SOUL

★ ★ ★ ★ ★

COUNTRY MUSIC HAS ALWAYS HAD A WAY OF SPEAKING FROM THE HEART and capturing the American spirit. From Dolly Parton's "I Will Always Love You" to Tim McGraw's "Live Like You Were Dying" and Zac Brown Band's "Chicken Fried," it's a genre unlike any other. It's a way of life—created by artists who pour themselves into the music they make, accompanied by the comforting sounds of steel guitars and soaring fiddles. And since every song tells a story, you just know country music is chock-full of good advice.

Everything I Need to Know I Learned from Country Music showcases more than sixty of these timeless tunes and the lessons they teach us about living life, loving well, working hard, and enjoying the simple things. If you don't already know these songs by heart, just think of this as your personal country music playlist. There's no time like the present to listen up and learn a thing or two!

Home isn't any one place in particular. It's the feeling of cool grass beneath your feet, of enjoying a home-cooked meal with family, and of raising a glass with friends at the end of a hard day's work. It's a way of life in small towns and wide-open spaces with only the sun on the horizon. And it's a focus on faith and tradition that's balanced out by simple pleasures and easy smiles.

Down home, high-school sweethearts, hard-won lessons, starry nights, and a tendency to tell it like it is are all as common as crickets chirping in the yard. It's the home that John Denver sings about in "Rocky Mountain High," that Kacey Musgraves sings about in "Merry Go 'Round," and that Lady A sings about in "Champagne Night." No matter where you call home yourself, the songs in this section speak to the home that's in your heart.

“YOU DON’T SEE
NO CITY
WHEN YOU LOOK
AT ME ’CAUSE
COUNTRY’S
ALL I AM”

YOU'RE LOOKIN' AT COUNTRY

Performed by Loretta Lynn

ONE THING ABOUT LEGENDARY COUNTRY CROONERS LIKE LORETTA LYNN: they know who they are and what they're about. Loretta's "You're Lookin' at Country" is a love letter to the sense of home, hard work, and happiness that she feels in the country. And it's encouraging the audience to embrace who they are and what they want. When you grow up running through cornfields and sharing farm-fresh suppers with family and friends, those things come to hold a special place in your heart.

BEHIND THE MUSIC ▶ *At the time, the song was a real departure for Loretta, who had famously done quite a bit of writing about bad husbands and broken hearts. But she told the compilation producer of her 1994 box set, Jimmy Guterman, that she was inspired to write what she saw for this song: her land. Framing the piece as a love song was a conscious choice that bridged the gap and helped it become one of Loretta's hallmarks. "You're Lookin' at Country" made it all the way to No. 5 on Billboard's "Hot Country Singles" chart in 1971.*

GIRL IN A COUNTRY SONG

Performed by Maddie & Tae

BACK IN THE OLD DAYS, YOU COULD COUNT ON COUNTRY SINGERS to put on the southern charm and paint a loving picture of the women in their lives. Even breakup songs were reverent and respectful. But when Maddie & Tae came out with this brutally honest hit, country music was overrun with songs that treated women like clichés of a country girl. Its lyrics don't pull any punches, directly referencing a number of these so-called "bro-country" songs performed by popular male artists. With an accompanying video that turns the tables on its male stars, the subversive song reminds us that people can't be limited to stereotypes. They're as varied and complicated as this country's multifaceted terrain.

BEHIND THE MUSIC ▶ *Radio programmers found the female artists' perspective refreshing and added the single to playlists typically filled with the tired tropes it calls out. In fact, "Girl in a Country Song" became Maddie & Tae's first No. 1 hit. It was only the second time in history a female duo had reached the top spot.*

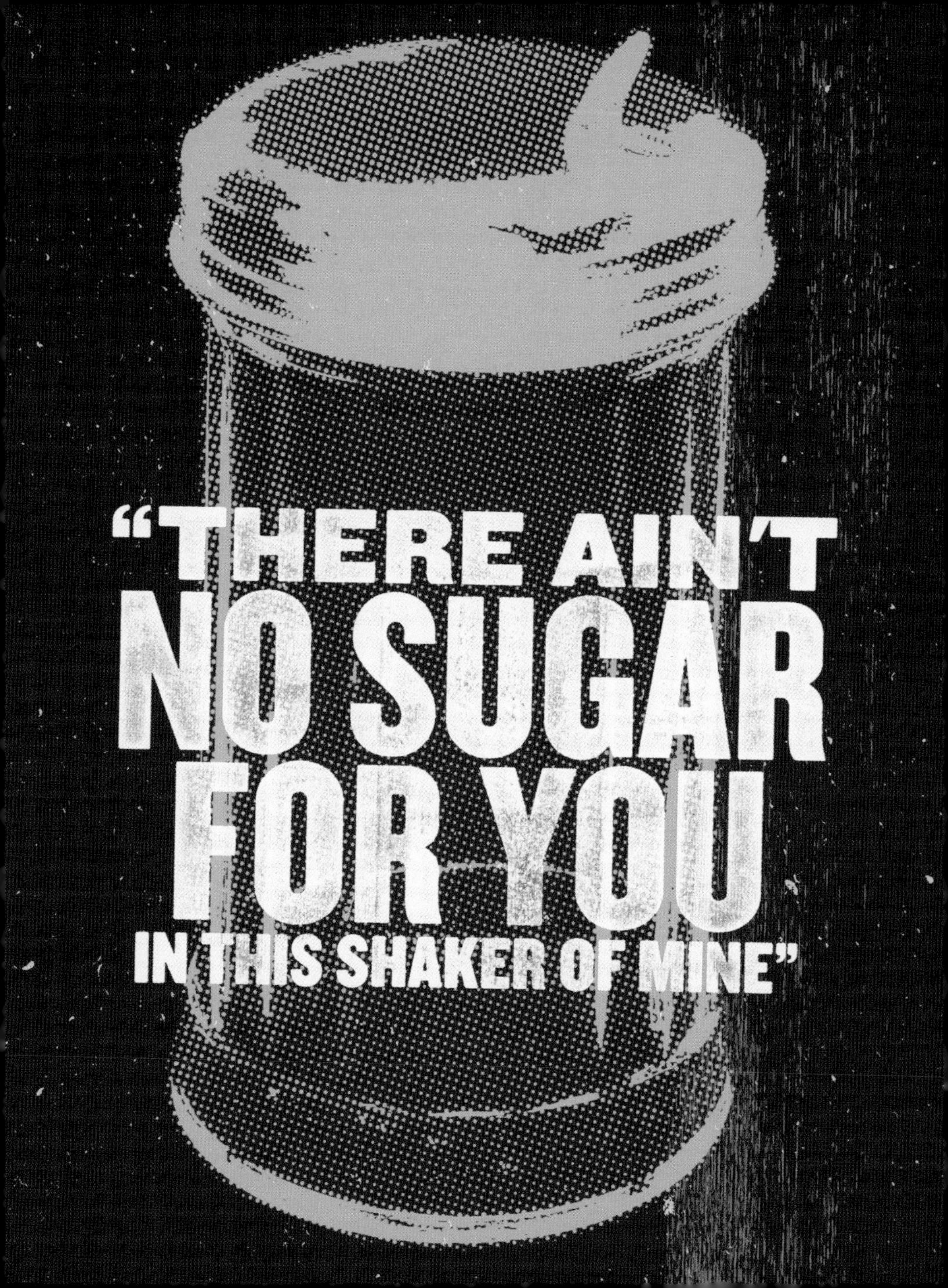"THERE AIN'T
NO SUGAR
FOR YOU
IN THIS SHAKER OF MINE"

"JUST WALKIN' THROUGH THE FRONT DOOR PUTS A BIG SMILE ON MY FACE"

I LOVE THIS BAR

Performed by Toby Keith

HOME IS THE PLACE WHERE YOU CAN BE YOURSELF. And to a lot of folks, like Toby Keith, the local bar is as close to home as it gets. It's the great equalizer, where all kinds can come as they are and enjoy a drink or two (or four), some company, and the great American pastime of people-watching. Whether you're feeling happy, lonesome, bored, or hopeful, connecting with people over a cold one is sometimes the best remedy for just about any problem. That's exactly why Toby chose to celebrate the local watering hole in his first single from his album *Shock'n Y'all.*

BEHIND THE MUSIC ▶ *Cowritten with Scotty Emerick, "I Love This Bar" held the top spot on Billboard's "Hot Country Singles & Tracks" chart for five weeks in 2003. And Billboard magazine's Ray Waddell wisely called it a "beer-joint staple for years to come." It even inspired a restaurant: Toby Keith's I Love This Bar & Grill. Although he lent his name to the venture, Toby has said he's happy to stick to music. And with a long track record of relatable songs like this one, his fans should be happy to hear it.*

MAY WE ALL

Performed by Florida Georgia Line and Tim McGraw

FROM DIRT ROADS AND BEAT-UP TRUCKS TO YOUNG LOVE and high-school football games, there's a lot to love about country living. The second single on an album appropriately titled *Dig Your Roots*, "May We All" is a celebration of the simple life, second chances, and the lessons they have to teach us. The heart-pounding video about risk-taking gone wrong during a car race brings the message home: Don't take a minute of those everyday pleasures for granted. They could be gone in the blink of an eye or the twist of a steering wheel.

BEHIND THE MUSIC ▶ *The song's writers, Rodney Clawson and Jamie Moore, told* Taste of Country *they tapped into their own small-town southern upbringings for the lyrics. Rodney and Jamie originally meant the song for Tim McGraw, but Florida Georgia Line snapped it up. And then they shrewdly asked the country music superstar and veteran actor to join the project.*

"MAY WE ALL
GET TO HAVE A CHANCE
TO RIDE THE FAST ONE
WALK AWAY WISER
WHEN WE CRASHED ONE"

"I WANNA LOOK AT THE HORIZON AND NOT SEE A BUILDING STANDING TALL"

COWBOY TAKE ME AWAY

Performed by The Chicks

IT'S EASY TO GET CAUGHT UP IN THE FLOW OF LIFE, your eyes never leaving a screen to look up at the horizon or the wild blue sky. But deep down, the country calls to you. You need its quiet calm to comfort you as much as you need to inhale deep lungfuls of its fresh, earth-scented air. "Cowboy Take Me Away" reminds you that sometimes you need to unplug, leave the city lights behind, and get back to your roots.

BEHIND THE MUSIC ▶ *Martie Maguire was inspired to write the song for her younger sister (and fellow Chicks member) Emily Strayer's upcoming wedding to country singer Charlie Robison. Martie's cowriter on the song, Marcus Hummon, told* The Tennessean *that it came together quickly over a shared meal of canned spaghetti. Martie's vision for the wild and beautiful life her sister could have resonated deeply with fans. In 2000, the year the song was released, The Chicks won the Academy of Country Music's Top Vocal Duo or Group of the Year award, Country Music Awards' Entertainer of the Year award, and both the ACM and CMA's Album of the Year awards.*

CHAMPAGNE NIGHT

Performed by Lady A

LADY A KNOWS HOW TO DO A NIGHT ON THE TOWN RIGHT.
Out in the country, it's all about keeping it real and marking life's
occasions with a no-frills good time. Sure, fancy can be fun sometimes.
But a hometown good time beats the VIP treatment every time. There's
nothing like wearing blue jeans and drinking cheap beer out of plastic
cups with friends who accept you for who you are. And that's what you
get down home—people who are just happy to be with you, bottle service
or no bottle service.

BEHIND THE MUSIC ▶ *When the song quickly climbed to number one, the
members of Lady A told* Billboard *they were thrilled that the lyrics resonated with
fans. The first radio single to come from NBC's songwriting competition* Songland,
*"Champagne Night" started out as contestant Madeline Merlo's "I'll Drink to That."
The trio worked with her and show mentor Shane McAnally to transform the song
into a chart-topping hit.*

"NO VELVET ROPES IN OUR HOMETOWN BAR OUR VIPS ARE DRINKIN' PBR"

"MAY BE A SIMPLE LIFE, BUT THAT'S OKAY IF YOU ASK ME BABY, I THINK I GOT IT MADE"

ALRIGHT

Performed by Darius Rucker

DARIUS RUCKER SURPRISED A LOT OF PEOPLE when he went from leading famous American rock band Hootie & the Blowfish to climbing the country-music charts. But he's clearly a country singer at heart, and this song about life, love, and gratitude proves it. After decades in the spotlight, Darius has probably enjoyed his fair share of five-star reservations and Dom Perignon. But, like his fellow country singers, he knows that the best things in life don't come with a big price tag. From home-cooked food and good company to lifelong love and a sense of belonging, the simple life is full of riches that some of the wealthiest people can only imagine.

BEHIND THE MUSIC ▶ *Darius collaborated on the song with Frank Rogers after the pair wrote "All I Want" together. "Alright" turns that song's story of divorce on its head with a lesson about appreciating all the blessings you have in front of you, including love. Despite some reviewers being critical of the song, it struck a chord with fans and became Darius's third number-one single on the country charts.*

ROCKY MOUNTAIN HIGH

Performed by John Denver

JOHN DENVER HAD A WAY WITH WORDS that turned lyrics into poetry and songs into stories you just have to hear again and again. The fiery sunsets, quieting starlight, and serene lakes of "Rocky Mountain High" would inspire any weary traveler or homesick cowgirl or boy. The lyrics of this song offer the comforting reassurance that you can find grace and a sense of belonging in wide-open, natural spaces even when you're far from home. But the story behind the song also proves that you can make a new home for yourself in whatever place inspires you.

BEHIND THE MUSIC ▶ *John wrote "Rocky Mountain High" three years after moving to Aspen, Colorado, and being awed by its spectacular sights. While testifying in Congress against censorship of the song for allegedly promoting substance abuse, he described the "elation," "celebration of life," and "joy in living" he felt while sharing the stunning beauty of a meteor shower on a moonless night with friends. John followed his heart to the Rockies and found a home there. And thirty-five years after he released his loving tribute, "Rocky Mountain High" became one of two official state songs of Colorado.*

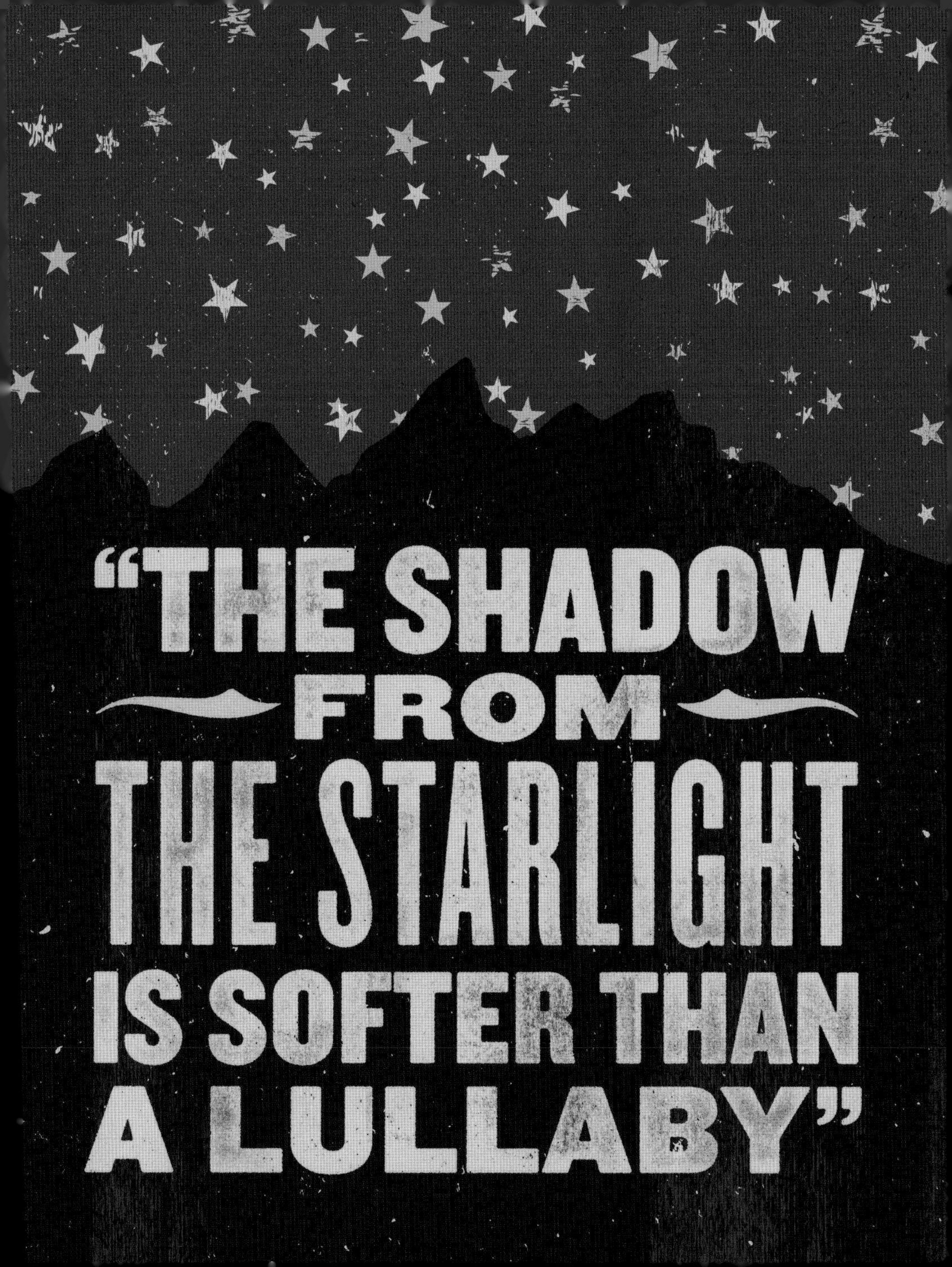
"THE SHADOW
FROM
THE STARLIGHT
IS SOFTER THAN
A LULLABY"

"JUST LIKE DUST
WE SETTLE
IN THIS TOWN"

MERRY GO 'ROUND

Performed by Kacey Musgraves

AS KACEY POINTS OUT IN THIS DARK PORTRAYAL OF SMALL-TOWN LIFE, the comfort of home isn't always all it's cracked up to be. Its traditions and expectations can be just as smothering for some as they are appealing for others. And recognizing which camp you fall into can be the difference between settling for good enough and going after what you really want. The lesson here is that there's no shame in getting off the merry go 'round if it doesn't suit you. In fact, it might end up being an incredible, life-changing choice.

BEHIND THE MUSIC ▶ *If you're tempted to stay in your comfort zone, Kacey wants you to know that you're not alone. She told* American Songwriter *she thinks "there's hope in knowing that everyone has felt this way." Everyone is figuring out their own way forward. For her part, Kacey followed her arrow from a small, conservative Texas town to Nashville to become an award-winning musician and an outspoken advocate for inclusivity.*

RAISED ON COUNTRY

Performed by Chris Young

COUNTRY MUSIC HAS CHANGED A LOT OVER THE YEARS, but its roots run deep. Those songs and the lessons they impart about living and loving have been passed down like family traditions. Just like Chris and cowriters Corey Crowder and Cary Barlowe, a lot of listeners were raised on Merle and Willie. That sense of connection and common ground? That's what country music is all about.

BEHIND THE MUSIC ▶ *Chris went all out to drive that connection home with "Raised on Country." In addition to dropping the names of several country greats in the lyrics, he filmed the song's video at the legendary WSM radio station—the birthplace of the Grand Ole Opry—where those greats were fixtures. A member of the Opry himself, Chris told* Rolling Stone *he was honored to film "where songs from my musical icons have played over the years." He's keeping the tradition of country music alive and well.*

"IT'S THE SOUNDTRACK TO MY LIFE IT RUNS DEEP IN MY DNA"

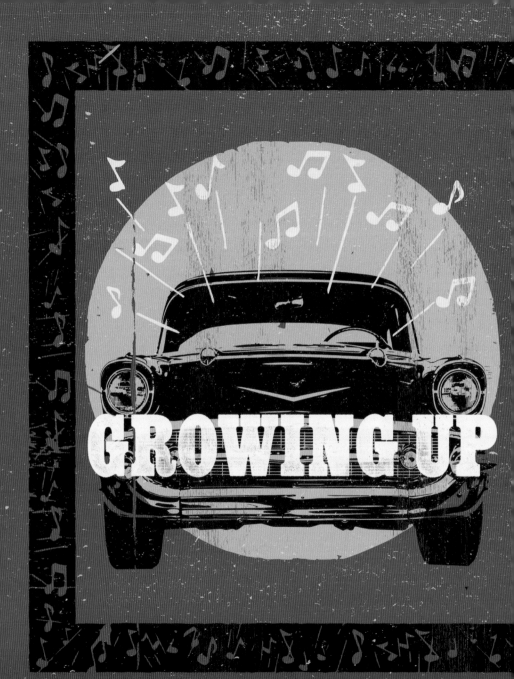

GROWING UP

Growing up isn't easy, but at least you know country music will be with you every step of the way. If you've lived it, a country musician has sung about it. You can find tracks with time-tested advice on everything from first crushes to crashed cars, bullies to big decisions, and graduation days to getting older. And a little guitar helps the message go down.

Let Faith Hill talk you through those wild teenage years with "Wild One," Hunter Hayes make you feel seen with "Invisible," and Trace Adkins help you keep some perspective with "You're Gonna Miss This." Whether they're telling the stories of days gone by or of what's yet to come, the songs in this section are all about growing into the person you hope to be—and taking your time doing it. Life, like country music, is all about savoring every sweet moment.

"you're gonna wish

THESE DAYS

hadn't gone by

SO FAST"

YOU'RE GONNA MISS THIS

Performed by Trace Adkins

WHEN YOU LOOK BACK ON YOUR LIFE, there are surely some moments in time you want to go back to (and others you're happy to leave in the past). But it's hard to recognize those moments as they happen. You get caught up living life or working toward your future, or you just get impatient for the next step. And before you know it, the moment's gone. "You're Gonna Miss This" is the reminder every country fan needs to slow down and enjoy the good times as they come.

BEHIND THE MUSIC ▶ *This song's message resonated with Trace, as the father of five daughters himself, and also with the song's writers. Songwriter Ashley Gorley told* Nash Country Weekly *that the verse describing a chaotic scene with an understanding plumber was inspired by his own children running circles around a repairman who answered Ashley's apology with "Don't worry about it—I've got two babies of my own." Cowriter Lee Thomas Miller came up with the song's title from there, and the pair worked backward to fill out the remaining lyrics. Together, the three men created a chart-topping hit that every fan can relate to.*

WILD ONE

Performed by Faith Hill

WHEN YOUR LITTLE ONES AREN'T SO LITTLE ANYMORE
and they're starting to make their own way in the world, it can be so
tempting to hold on tight. But the harder you do, the more they'll fight to
run free. "Wild One" gets right to the heart of that teenage tug-of-war,
reminding parents that when you encourage your babies to dream big,
you don't get to choose what they dream of. You have to let go and let
them be the amazing people you raised them to be.

BEHIND THE MUSIC ▶ *Having been adopted just a few days after her
birth, Faith felt that struggle herself at times growing up. Her adoptive family
was encouraging, but they didn't share Faith's passion for music. "I had a spirit
completely outside what my family was," she told Billboard. But because of her
birth mother's sacrifice and her adoptive family's love, Faith was able to achieve
her dream of becoming a country music icon. "Wild One" was her first number-one
single, holding the top spot for four weeks.*

"SHE HAS FUTURE PLANS AND DREAMS AT NIGHT"

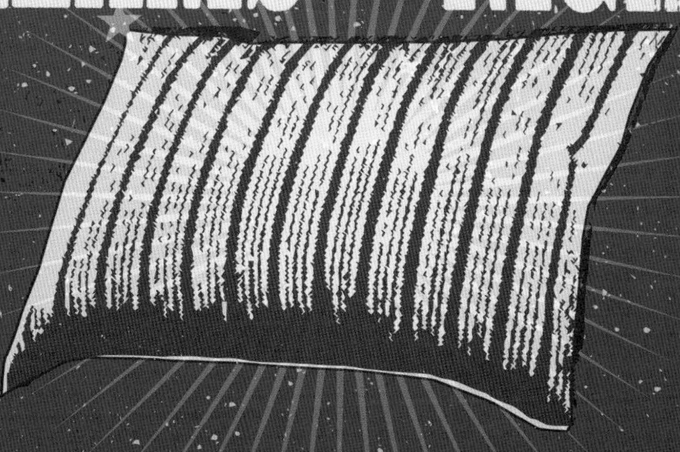

"THESE ARE NOWHERE NEAR THE BEST YEARS OF YOUR LIFE"

LETTER TO ME

Performed by Brad Paisley

IF YOU COULD WRITE A LETTER TO YOUR SEVENTEEN-YEAR-OLD SELF, what would it say? Would you fill it with regrets, or with reassurance? As usual, Brad Paisley hits the nail on the head with his insightful song "Letter to Me." Between school and life and first loves, teenagers have a lot of competing pressures. They need compassion and encouragement. They need to hear that it's okay to struggle, that things will get easier. And sometimes, adults need to hear it, too.

BEHIND THE MUSIC ▶ *At the 2018 Country Radio Seminar, Brad said that he never intended for the song to be a single, let alone a hit. He just "knew it needed to exist." But he also said he finds that, while many of the folks in Nashville focus on trying to make songs that sell, it's songs that tell the truth that resonate with fans the most. "Letter to Me" won Brad the award for Best Male Country Vocal Performance at the 51st Grammy Awards.*

INVISIBLE

Performed by Hunter Hayes

IF YOU'VE EVER BEEN BULLIED, FELT ALONE, OR WANTED TO FADE INTO THE BACKGROUND, Hunter Hayes wants you to know you're not alone. With "Invisible," he hopes to reach people who are hurting to tell them that there are brighter days ahead. So, dare to be different, to march to your own heartbeat, and to step into the light. Standing out from the crowd can be a huge blessing when you learn to embrace it.

BEHIND THE MUSIC ▶ *When Hunter sat down to write the song with Katrina Elam and Bonnie Baker, he told USA Today, they were intent on writing an up-tempo love song. But as they got to talking, the conversation turned to bullying. When Katrina talked about moments of feeling invisible, something clicked for Hunter and Bonnie. Each cowriter added their own experiences of feeling lonely or left out. But rather than focus on the loneliness, they created a song that they hoped would empower listeners to live authentically.*

"EVERY **HEART** HAS A RHYTHM — LET YOURS **BEAT** OUT SO LOUDLY"

"WHAT I WOULDN'T GIVE TO BE TWENTY-ONE, WILD AND FREE"

SIXTEEN

Performed by Thomas Rhett

BY THE TIME HE WROTE "SIXTEEN" AT THE WISE OLD AGE OF TWENTY-FIVE, Thomas Rhett had already learned to live in the moment. This look back at his younger self is a lesson for anyone trying to turn pages on the calendar a little too quickly. Just because the grass seems greener a few miles down the road doesn't mean you need to be in a hurry to get there. When you're focused on the next big milestone, it's easy to miss the perks of your current stage of life. You'll get where you want to go in time, so just sit back and enjoy the ride.

BEHIND THE MUSIC ▶ *Thomas's easygoing self-awareness didn't just help him stay grounded during the years of success that followed: it helped him achieve that success in the first place by inspiring a number of relatable, lighthearted hits like this one. Just as he did in his 2015 chart topper "Die a Happy Man" (which he also cowrote with Joe Spargur and Sean Douglas), Thomas lets his life lessons speak for themselves in "Sixteen."*

RED DIRT ROAD

Performed by Brooks & Dunn

FOR KIX BROOKS AND RONNIE DUNN (AND A LOT OF COUNTRY STARS), growing up in the country meant growing up in faith. It's just as much a part of who they are as their first beer, first love, and first time leaving home. "Red Dirt Road" reminds you that you might lose sight of your faith at times just like you do your hometown. You may even run from it. But when you reach for it again, you'll find it's waiting to welcome you back like a long-lost friend and carry you through all of life's ups and downs.

BEHIND THE MUSIC ▶ *In an interview for Phil Vassar's* Songs from the Cellar, *Kix admitted that the idea to call Brooks & Dunn's eighth album* Red Dirt Road *came before the iconic duo had written a single lyric for the song. They had just got to talking about their grandparents and growing up along those rural roads. When they sat down to write, recalling the best and worst of their childhood memories, the song came together within hours.*

"I LEARNED THE PATH TO HEAVEN IS FULL OF SINNERS AND BELIEVERS"

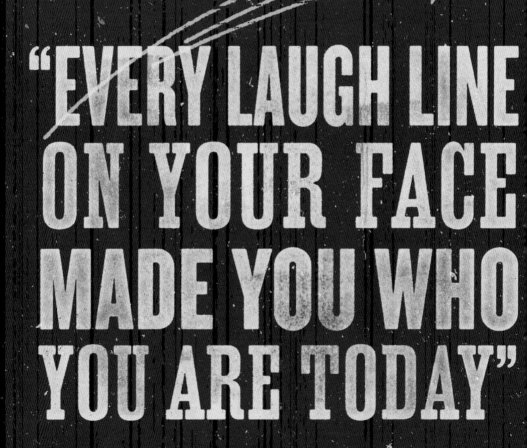

"EVERY LAUGH LINE ON YOUR FACE MADE YOU WHO YOU ARE TODAY"

THIS ONE'S FOR THE GIRLS

Performed by Martina McBride

GROWING UP CAN BRING WITH IT A LOT OF INSECURITY
AND HEARTACHE—especially for girls. In addition to bullies, broken
hearts, and the weight of big dreams, women young and old face some
pretty high (and often unrealistic) expectations. This empowering
anthem is here to let them know that not only are they not alone, but
that they also have nothing to prove. Just as it was intended to, the
song resonates with women of all ages. No matter where you are in life
or what you've faced, it always feels good to be reminded that you're
beautiful the way you are, and that you've got this.

BEHIND THE MUSIC ▶ *This song's positive message is one Martina
immediately knew she could get behind. She told* Billboard *that recording the song
was "an immediate no-brainer." In that same interview, she said that "This One's
for the Girls" is still one of her favorites to perform live nearly fifteen years after
its release because "it's like a shot of energy that goes through the crowd."*

THE IMPOSSIBLE

Performed by Joe Nichols

EVEN IN COUNTRY MUSIC, GROWING UP ISN'T ALL
FIREFLIES AND FIRST LOVES. You'll find some hard lessons laid
out in lyric form. But songs like "The Impossible" show you how those
hard lessons prepare you for life and teach you to keep going when
things get tough. Dealing with the death of a loved one, seeing your
unbreakable dad break down, watching a friend go through hell and beat
the odds—you go through it all so that you can come out on the other
side, stronger and wiser.

BEHIND THE MUSIC ▶ *According to a Tennessean interview with songwriters
Lee Thomas Miller and Kelley Lovelace, the song wasn't always so inspirational.
It focused more on the broken than the unbreakable. When the song's publisher
encouraged the duo to write something more uplifting, they created the story of
Billy. Little did they know, a young man was about to live those lyrics. Billy "Trey"
Howell III woke from his coma after a terrible car wreck remembering almost
nothing except a favorite song: "The Impossible." The songwriters' words inspired
him to fight to walk again.*

"'CAUSE THERE'S NO SUCH THING AS HOPELESS IF YOU BELIEVE"

MY WISH

Performed by Rascal Flatts

WITH LYRICS EVERY PARENT FEELS IN THEIR BONES, "My Wish" is more of a blessing than it is a song. Listening to the lyrics puts into perspective what's really important when you're raising kids. More than anything, you want them to grow up to be happy and fulfilled and to know that you always have their backs. Becoming who they're meant to be might take a bit of resilience and a lot of trial and error. But knowing their parents love and support them can make all the difference.

BEHIND THE MUSIC ▶ *"My Wish" was inspired by songwriter Jeffrey Steele's thirteen-year-old daughter. According to an interview with The Boot, Justine Steele accused her dad of only writing songs for her older sisters. When cowriter Steve Robson began to play the music he'd written that same day, Jeffrey heard himself sing, "I hope the days come easy and the moments pass slow" and knew he had something special—a song for Justine, but also for parents everywhere.*

"I HOPE THE DAYS COME EASY AND THE MOMENTS PASS SLOW"

"REMEMBER WHEN THIRTY SEEMED SO OLD NOW LOOKIN' BACK, IT'S JUST A STEPPIN' STONE"

REMEMBER WHEN

Performed by Alan Jackson

ONE THING PEOPLE MIGHT NOT REALIZE ABOUT
RELATIONSHIPS—especially those that start out early on in life—is
how much growing up you do together. Depending on how you handle
it, all that change can make you stronger or it can break you up. Alan
Jackson knows that firsthand. "Remember When" was inspired by his
real lifelong love with his wife, Denise. From the first spark of young
love to the sound of little feet, and then letting go when the time comes,
this beautiful story takes the long view of their relationship. "Remember
When" is a lesson from the Jacksons in living, learning, and appreciating
all the good times you had while you were growing up together.

BEHIND THE MUSIC ▶ *Teenage sweethearts, Alan and Denise have seen it
all on their journey from the Georgia Dairy Queen where they met in high school
to Nashville's Country Music Hall of Fame. And as the song says, they experienced
plenty of joy and hurt along the way, including struggles with infidelity and cancer.
But the pair found their way back to each other through love and faith.*

GOOD TIMES

Work hard, play hard" might as well be country music's motto. These folks know how to have a good time. From crowding around a bonfire with a can of something in their hand to driving with the top down on a country road or warming the bottoms of their feet in sun-soaked sand, country musicians have found countless ways to enjoy themselves.

Country music can make you think that "good time" is synonymous with "party." And sure, there are plenty of songs (like Blake Shelton's "All About Tonight") you can take at face value. But you also don't have to dig too deep to see the best times have little to do with drinking the night away. From old friends reminiscing in Eric Church's "Talladega" to hood-slidin' nights in Dierks Bentley's "What Was I Thinkin'" and covert kisses in Scotty McCreery's "Five More Minutes," the songs in this section will have you raising a glass to a life well lived.

"IT DON'T TAKE BUT TWO TO HAVE A LITTLE SOIREE"

HOUSE PARTY

Performed by Sam Hunt

SAM HUNT KNOWS THE SECRET TO A GOOD TIME: You don't need bonfires, pontoon boats, or margaritas to get this soiree started. A good friend, some cold beer, and a couple of decent speakers will do the trick. The lesson here is to keep things simple. You could also learn from the narrator's mistakes: instead of making the neighbors hate you, invite them to the party!

BEHIND THE MUSIC ▶ *Although the lyrics are all about having a good time, coming up with them wasn't an easy task. Sam has a reputation in Nashville for perfectionism, working relentlessly until a song is everything he wants it to be. And "House Party" was no exception. He spent several sessions fine-tuning the song with Zach Crowell and Jerry Flowers, who told* Taste of Country, *"I think that's why his stuff is really connecting to so many people, because he doesn't stop until it's great." His hard work paid off with this platinum hit.*

NO SHOES, NO SHIRT, NO PROBLEMS

Performed by Kenny Chesney

LOVING THE ROLLING HILLS, WIDE-OPEN FIELDS, and rushing rivers of the American countryside doesn't mean you can't appreciate having your toes in the sand, and no one knows that better than Kenny Chesney. When he's not recording or out on tour, there's a good chance you'll find him soaking up the sun somewhere tropical. With "No Shoes, No Shirt, No Problems," he reminds you that it's okay to relax and forget your troubles sometimes. If you can't make it to the beach, just take a few minutes to put your feet up, hit "play," and let this laid-back tune wash over you.

BEHIND THE MUSIC ▶ *When songwriter Casey Beathard played him a few bars of the song, which wasn't finished at the time, Kenny knew it was for him. In an interview for* The Tennessean's *"Story Behind the Song," Casey recalled him saying, "Man, that's where I am right now in my life . . . that's me." He told Casey to finish it up and send it over. Thanks to Kenny and Casey, songs with island vibes started to fill the country airwaves.*

"WANT TO SOAK UP LIFE
FOR A WHILE IN
LAID BACK MODE"

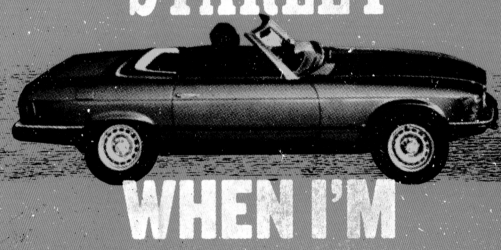

'80S MERCEDES

Performed by Maren Morris

MAREN'S REALLY ONTO SOMETHING WITH "'80S MERCEDES"—when it comes to a good time, it's not about what you have but how it makes you feel. And you don't need a fancy car to feel good. All you need is to throw on some shades and roll the windows down on a long, scenic stretch of highway. While you're at it, tune the radio to the classic country station. Some good music and a little warm air on your skin will take you right back to teenage dreams and carefree Saturday nights.

BEHIND THE MUSIC ▶ *Maren wrote both "'80s Mercedes" and another hit, "My Church," in the same week, telling iHeart that she must have just been in a car-driving mood at the time. But she wanted the songs to play off each other, too. "'80s Mercedes" was the Saturday-night twist to the Sunday-morning feeling of "My Church." Both celebrate how music can move you. And if it moves you to feel as good as this hit does, all the better.*

TALLADEGA

Performed by Eric Church

HAVING A DRINK AND BLOWING OFF SOME STEAM CAN MAKE FOR A GOOD TIME, but the best times are the ones that bring a smile to your face years later. Fishing with your grandpa, staying out with your buddies 'til the sun comes up, taking your little ones for tractor rides—these are the scenes that'll play through your mind when you get to the end of the road. You don't always know a memory in the making, so take your cue from "Talladega" and make the most of every incredible moment.

BEHIND THE MUSIC ▶ *Eric Church told ESPN reporter Marty Smith (who's proud to call Eric his best friend) that "Talladega" is simply "magic." The song took Eric and cowriter Luke Laird just two hours to write, coming together like it was meant to be. It's more than a song about NASCAR. In fact, to a lot of people, it's not about NASCAR at all. It's about those moments in life that you know are special, that you'll keep with you and look back on fondly.*

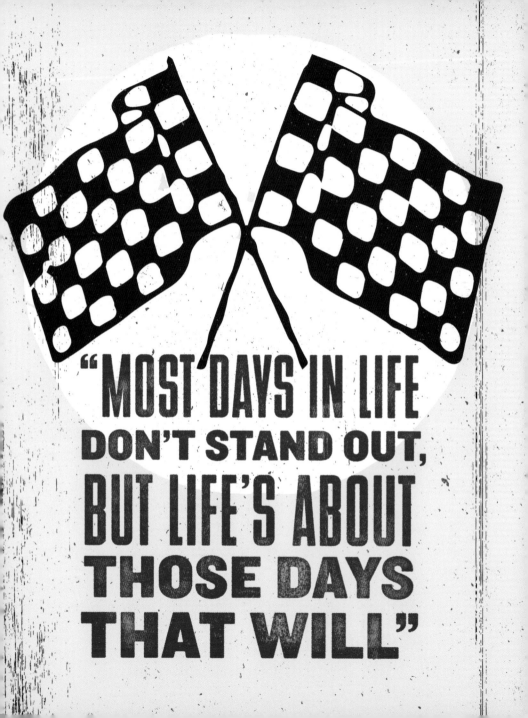

"MOST DAYS IN LIFE DON'T STAND OUT, BUT LIFE'S ABOUT THOSE DAYS THAT WILL"

"CAN'T BEAT THE HEAT

SO LET'S TAKE A RIDE"

PONTOON

Performed by Little Big Town

WHAT DO YOU DO WHEN A COLD BEER ISN'T ENOUGH TO COOL YOU DOWN on a hot day? You take the party down to the water! Following in the sun-soaked footsteps of Craig Morgan's "Redneck Yacht Club," "Pontoon" is the summer anthem of country fans who know that some blue mountains, black inner tubes, and good attitudes can save any sweltering day. The lesson here is clear: You can turn any situation into a good time if you just get a little creative.

BEHIND THE MUSIC ▶ *Songwriter Natalie Hemby is responsible for bringing the party to pontoon boats everywhere. According to an interview with The Boot, it was all in good fun. Natalie learned that someone misheard the title of Miranda Lambert's "Fine Tune" and found the mistake hilarious. Together with Luke Laird and Barry Dean, she turned the error into what would become Little Big Town's first number-one single.*

ALL ABOUT TONIGHT

Performed by Blake Shelton

THERE ARE COUNTRY SONGS THAT LAMENT THE PAST and country songs that look toward the future, but some of the best lessons come from songs like this one that are about living in the moment. When your week is nothing but long days, "All About Tonight" is a much-needed reminder to make the most of a good night. Just make sure you do what you need to do to feel as good the next morning as you did the night before. (A few electrolytes can go a long way.)

BEHIND THE MUSIC ▶ *According to an interview with* The Boot, *songwriters Rhett Akins, Dallas Davidson, and Ben Hayslip (collectively known as The Peach Pickers) just wanted to write a fun song about living it up for the night. Rhett, who had worked with Blake Shelton on several other songs, knew he'd be the perfect artist to bring it to life. The song became the title track of Blake's second extended play and his seventh number-one hit.*

"TOOK A DIRT ROAD AND HAD THE RADIO BLASTIN'"

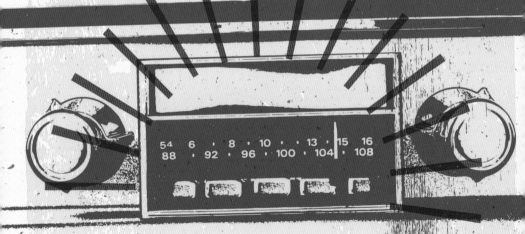

WHAT WAS
I THINKIN'

Performed by Dierks Bentley

SOME OF THE BEST TIMES IN YOUR LIFE ARE GOING TO BE
THE ONES THAT YOU PROBABLY SHOULD HAVE AVOIDED. But
what's life without a little risk? Most times, it's worth the reward.
Sometimes, like when someone's waving a 12-gauge at you, it's really not.
But Dierks (alongside Brett Beavers and Deric Ruttan) perfectly captures
the feeling of getting caught up in that moment and throwing caution—and
personal safety—to the wind. As a country star, Dierks is living the lesson
of "What Was I Thinkin'": Take a risk. You may end up a little worse for
wear sometimes, but you'll come out of it with a hell of a story.

BEHIND THE MUSIC ▶ *Dierks told CMT that he moved to Nashville when he
was just nineteen years old, with dreams of being a performer. Making your way
in country music is no small feat, so he took odd jobs and played for small crowds
while he found his footing. It took him seven years to make his way over to Capitol
Records, but today he has more than two dozen hits and sings to sold-out arenas.*

DOWN IN MISSISSIPPI
(UP TO NO GOOD)

Performed by Sugarland

SOMETIMES, SELF-CARE LOOKS LIKE A HOT BATH AND
A GLASS OF WINE. Other times, it looks like best friends and a
blackjack table. The important thing is to make time for a good time
when you need it. And "Down in Mississippi" is preaching that lesson
to every overworked, fed up, and just-plain-exhausted woman within
earshot. So, the next time you feel a breakdown coming on, take a break
instead. And if that break takes you down to Mississippi, all the better.

BEHIND THE MUSIC ▶ *Inspired by wild nights on the newly opened riverboat
casinos, "Down in Mississippi" was the last single from the only album that
featured all three original members of Sugarland. Eventually, even the remaining
two, Kristian Bush and Jennifer Nettles, would go their own ways for a time. But
they came back from their hiatus better than ever, with fuller cups and a fresh
perspective on making music together.*

"NO MORE, WHAT A BORE, HAD ENOUGH, I'M OUT THE DOOR"

"THEN WE SAT AROUND 'TIL THE BREAK OF DAWN HOWLIN' and SINGIN' OUR FAVORITE SONGS"

BAREFOOT BLUE JEAN NIGHT

Performed by Jake Owen

WARM SUMMER NIGHTS SITTING BY THE FIRE WITH FRIENDS, drink in hand, looking up at a blanket of stars and singing along while someone strums an old guitar—there's nothing like it. When you're young, those barefoot blue jean nights feel like they'll never end. But don't let the nostalgia of nights gone by get you down. If you learn anything from Jake Owen's doing flips on the water in this song's video, it's that if it's in your heart, you can recapture that feeling at any age.

BEHIND THE MUSIC ▶ *The song's lightheartedness comes straight from songwriters Eric Paslay, Dylan Altman, and Terry Sawchuk. Eric told* Taste of Country, *"When we recorded the demo, you could hear that we were having a lot of fun with it. We weren't sweating over the song in any way." As an easygoing, sun-soaked Florida native, Jake was the perfect person to bring the trio's upbeat summertime anthem to life on the radio. Together, they created a song that keeps that carefree spirit alive.*

FIVE MORE MINUTES

Performed by Scotty McCreery

WHEN YOU LOOK BACK AT ALL THE GOOD TIMES YOU'VE HAD IN YOUR LIFE, the little things probably stand out as much as the big things. Catching lightning bugs with your big brother, making pies with your grandma, the good-night kiss after a first date. Like the boy in the song savoring his last time out on the field, the trick is appreciating the good times while they're happening. That way, your only regret when you look back is that you didn't have a few more minutes to enjoy them.

BEHIND THE MUSIC ▶ *"Five More Minutes" hit number one after a yearlong battle to wrangle it from the record label that dropped Scotty McCreery. He knew that fans would relate to the message of the song, which he cowrote with Frank Rogers and Monty Criswell. Scotty risked his career to get it in front of audiences, playing the song to standing ovations before he'd regained the rights. Fighting for it was the right choice, for both Scotty and his fans.*

"WISH I HAD ME A PAUSE BUTTON"

REAL LOVE

There's something about a country love story that beats all, maybe because it doesn't shy away from the hard stuff or gloss over the good stuff. A country love story is real, it's true, and it's not always what you think it is. Dolly Parton's "I Will Always Love You" is a testament to the purest kind of love—the wish to see another person happy without you—and she wrote it about her business partner. Johnny Cash wrote "I Walk the Line" to keep himself on the straight and narrow when he was struggling. But then there are songs like Dan + Shay's "Speechless" that share the joy of finding your forever in another person.

The songs in this section cover all kinds of love, from the love of a family to the love of a soul mate, and even love for humanity. They're lofty, hopeful, endearing, and sometimes even heartbreaking, but they're always real. And they've got a lot to teach you if you're willing to listen.

"But above all this
I WISH YOU
LOVE"

I WILL ALWAYS LOVE YOU

Performed by Dolly Parton

DESPITE HAVING A REAL LIFELONG LOVE OF HER OWN with husband Carl Thomas Dean, Dolly Parton wrote one of the most romantic breakup songs of all time. "I Will Always Love You" is a touching tribute to the purest form of love: selfless love. When your wish for another person to feel joy and happiness overpowers your desire for that happiness to include you, you know it's real love. It may be bittersweet, but walking away might be the best thing you can do for your relationship.

BEHIND THE MUSIC ▶ *Dolly didn't actually write this song about a romantic relationship. She wrote it for friend and colleague Porter Wagoner, whose show she was getting ready to leave. Dolly told Bart Herbison of Nashville Songwriters Association International that Porter cried when he heard the song, and then he said, "Well, hell! If you feel that strong about it, just go on—providing I get to produce that record because that's the best song you ever wrote." He did, and the song hit number one three times: once when it was released in 1974, again when Dolly rerecorded it for the 1982 movie* The Best Little Whorehouse in Texas, *and finally in 1992, when Whitney Houston put her own incredible spin on it.*

YOU'RE MY BETTER HALF

Performed by Keith Urban

TAKE IT FROM KEITH: Love is even sweeter when you know you can count on each other. If you're fortunate enough to have a true partner by your side, someone who balances you out and brightens you up on good days and bad, thank your lucky stars. It's a rare gift. And if you haven't found it yet, don't stop looking until you do. Few things in life can match the magic of finding someone who will walk hand in hand with you through it all and make you believe you can make it through anything.

BEHIND THE MUSIC ▶ *With the well-known love story between Keith and Nicole Kidman, it's easy to assume that he and cowriter John Shanks wrote this song for her. But the two didn't meet until a year after the song's 2004 release. Still, their relationship embodies the message of the song. They've both said in interviews that finding one another is the best thing that's ever happened to them. Their partnership has seen them through the good and the bad, including Keith's battle with addiction. But they're living these lyrics and facing life together.*

"I'D RATHER HAVE YOU BY MY SIDE"

"I KEEP YOU
ON MY MIND
BOTH DAY
AND NIGHT"

I WALK THE LINE

Performed by Johnny Cash

"I WALK THE LINE" MIGHT NOT BE THE LOVE SONG COUNTRY FANS THINK IT IS. When Johnny wrote "I find it very, very easy to be true," he wasn't saying that being loyal to his wife was easy. He walked the line between temptation and fidelity because he made a commitment to his wife, and he made the choice each day to abide by it. Between the women on tour and the amphetamines fed to the band by doctors, the temptation grew too strong; Johnny famously crossed that line. But that makes the song's lesson all the more compelling: Finding real love doesn't mean things will be easy. You have to keep a close watch on your heart every day.

BEHIND THE MUSIC ▶ *Johnny was just twenty-three years old and married to his first wife, Vivian, at the time he wrote "I Walk the Line." Touring with Elvis Presley meant being surrounded by adoring, attractive young women. In a 1997 interview with Terry Gross, he said that the song was "a kind of prodding to myself to 'play it straight, Johnny.'"*

YOU'RE STILL THE ONE

Performed by Shania Twain

AT THE BEGINNING, LOVE FEELS EXTRAORDINARY. After a few years together, though, it's all too easy to let the rhythm of ordinary life dull that feeling. You start to take your partner for granted and forget that, once upon a time, a life with them is all you ever wanted. Real love is hard won. Make sure you take the time to kiss each other good night and appreciate how far you've come since those early days. You've made it, and that's certainly something to be grateful for.

BEHIND THE MUSIC ▶ *Shania Twain wrote the song with her then-husband and producer Robert John "Mutt" Lange. Although the two have since divorced, Shania has said that "You're Still the One" remains one of her favorite songs to perform. In one of her most memorable performances, a live concert in Las Vegas, she sang the love song to an elegant white horse she rode out on stage. Shania wrote in her autobiography,* From This Moment On, *that the song came together like magic. It offers a bit of that magic to every lover who listens to it.*

"AIN'T NOTHING BETTER
WE BEAT THE ODDS
TOGETHER"

"AND I'VE BEEN IN A DAZE EVER SINCE THE DAY THAT WE MET"

SPEECHLESS

Performed by Dan + Shay

YOU KNOW YOU'VE FOUND THE REAL THING WHEN YOUR PARTNER STILL TAKES YOUR BREATH AWAY months, or even years, later. "Speechless" celebrates the exhilarating feeling of that once-in-a-lifetime love. It's a feeling that was fresh on the minds of Dan Smyers and Shay Mooney, who had both recently gotten married when they wrote the song. The song serves as a reminder to the country duo, as well as to their fans, to honor that kind of love. Whenever you find yourself speechless (in a good way), stop and drink in the scene. It's those little, breathless moments in time that form the memories you'll look back on together years down the road.

BEHIND THE MUSIC ▶ *When it came time to create the music video for "Speechless," Dan told PEOPLE he had a crazy idea: a mashup of the duo's elegant real-life country weddings. What could be a more perfect complement to the song's lyrics than seeing the moments when both singers fell speechless at the sight of their brides? Now the singers and their wives have another sweet memento of the day—one that Dan says he and his wife, Abby, enjoyed watching on their first anniversary.*

HOMESICK

Performed by Kane Brown

NO LOVE IS MORE REAL THAN THE LOVE YOU FEEL FOR YOUR FAMILY. And when you're away from them, you start to realize how much the little things matter. Dancing around the kitchen together, holding hands, whispering good night—it's like all that closeness stays put while you're apart and waits for you to come home to it. Leaving it means leaving a part of you behind. The only cure for that kind of homesick is to hold on tight to your loved ones and make the most of the time you have together, no matter how brief or how long.

BEHIND THE MUSIC ▶ *Kane Brown penned the song with Matthew McGinn, Brock Berryhill, and Taylor Phillips after leaving his then-fiancée to go on tour. His cowriters watched his anguish over missing calls and moments with her. Today, Kane leaves wife Katelyn Jae and their little ones behind when he heads out on the road. But they join him on tour as much as possible to soak up as many moments together as possible.*

"IF HOME IS WHERE THE HEART IS I'M HOMESICK FOR YOU"

"WHEN WE STAND TOGETHER IT'S OUR FINEST HOUR"

LOVE CAN BUILD A BRIDGE

Performed by The Judds

LEAVE IT TO THIS ICONIC MOTHER-DAUGHTER DUO to remind country fans that love is about more than romance and passion. Real love is a universal language, understood by every heart. Their song "Love Can Build a Bridge" is a call to start from a place of love with every person you encounter, healing the wounds of division and distrust through compassion and respect. More than anything, the song encourages listeners to have faith that love can change the world.

BEHIND THE MUSIC ▶ *Inspired by a conversation with cowriter Paul Overstreet, Naomi Judd wrote the song's lyrics and handed them over to John Barlow Jarvis. He told* Nashville Hype *that he instantly heard a melody and had the rest of the song written in just fifteen minutes. For such a quick collaboration, "Love Can Build a Bridge" has stood the test of time as a country classic and a message of hope. The song's message is as relevant today as it was back when The Judds recorded it in 1990.*

CHECK YES OR NO

Performed by George Strait

TALK ABOUT YOUNG LOVE! Not many people can say that they found their soul mate in third grade, let alone that their love is still going strong twenty years later. That's why this song has touched so many hearts since its debut in 1995—it's the kind of story that inspires you to open your own heart to the possibility of true love. Even if you didn't meet your partner early on, there's a lesson for you here: holding on to your childlike joy like these childhood sweethearts did might just be the key to making love last. Think back to how you were in the first days of your relationship and try to recreate that spark. A little bit of chasing could do you both a world of good.

BEHIND THE MUSIC ▶ *Clearly George Strait knows how to pick songs like the protagonist of this one knows how to pick partners. Written by Dana Hunt Black and Danny Wells, "Check Yes or No" was number twenty-eight of the more than sixty chart-topping hits George has enjoyed throughout his career.*

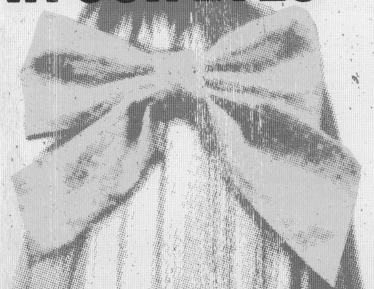

"STILL LIKE TWO KIDS ~WITH~ STARS IN OUR EYES"

"'CAUSE WE'VE GOT
— the kind of love —
PEOPLE DREAM ABOUT"

DON'T LET OUR LOVE START SLIPPIN' AWAY

Performed by Vince Gill

FOR A SONG THAT SPEAKS SO EARNESTLY ABOUT HOLDING ON TO LOVE, its upbeat tempo might take you by surprise. But "Don't Let Our Love Start Slippin' Away" is about having faith in the strength and resiliency of your relationship, and that's something to celebrate. That doesn't mean it's easy. As Vince sings, "real love walks a real fine line," and you can't just expect it to keep itself from falling. When life gets harder and love starts to teeter on that line, you've got to communicate and commit to working things out. At the end of the day, your love is worth more than any argument. So let go of who's right and who's wrong and just hold on to each other.

BEHIND THE MUSIC ▶ *To add to the fun, the song's video features an almost endless parade of country stars, including Little Jimmy Dickens, Patty Loveless, Kathy Mattea, Carl Perkins, Pam Tillis, and even Reba McEntire as a gum-smacking waitress. Together, they get everyone in the room dancing and having a good time.*

BEAUTIFUL CRAZY

Performed by Luke Combs

Only a country singer could find a way to call a woman crazy that actually endears female fans to them, and it's because you can feel the love behind the lyrics. Songs like this one show you that what you love most about someone are usually the little things that make them *them*. It's those little things that make "Beautiful Crazy" the kind of country love song that fans play over and over again. It also happens to be one of the singer's favorites. Not only did it win him Song of the Year at the 2019 Country Music Association Awards, but it also won him the heart and hand of his love, Nicole Hocking Combs.

BEHIND THE MUSIC ▶ *Luke wrote the song for Nicole and shared it with her before the two were even dating in what he calls "a baller move." Although he told podcaster Lindsay Czarniak that Nicole played it cool in the moment, hearing someone sing about all the things that make them a fool for you is enough to make anyone swoon. Like countless couples since, Luke and Nicole chose "Beautiful Crazy" for the first dance at their wedding.*

"WELL, IT KINDA SCARES ME THE WAY THAT SHE DRIVES ME WILD"

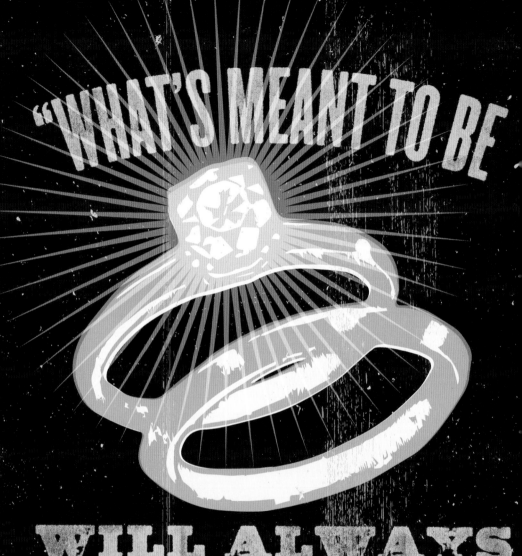

SHE'S IN LOVE WITH THE BOY

Performed by Trisha Yearwood

"SHE'S IN LOVE WITH THE BOY" IS A GOOD LESSON for anyone thinking they can stand in the way of what's meant to be. Like young Katie in this song, love has a mind of its own. You can't control it. And it certainly doesn't give a lick about anyone else's opinion of it. If you're outside looking in on someone else's love, don't fool yourself into thinking you can change it. There's no use losing your temper about other people's relationships, and that's a surefire way to cause trouble for yourself. Instead, have the sense to let it play out, and just be there to pick up the pieces if it falls apart or to celebrate if it stands the test of time.

BEHIND THE MUSIC ▶ *When Trisha Yearwood chose to record John Ims's "She's in Love with the Boy," she picked it just because she liked it (and because she had some experience being daddy's little girl). But then the song made country-music history as the first debut single by a female artist to hit number one. While Trisha was excited to hold the honor, she quickly felt the pressure to prove she wasn't just a one-hit wonder. Clearly, she rose to the occasion. Today, Trisha has nine number-one singles as well as a number of Grammy, CMA, and ACM awards.*

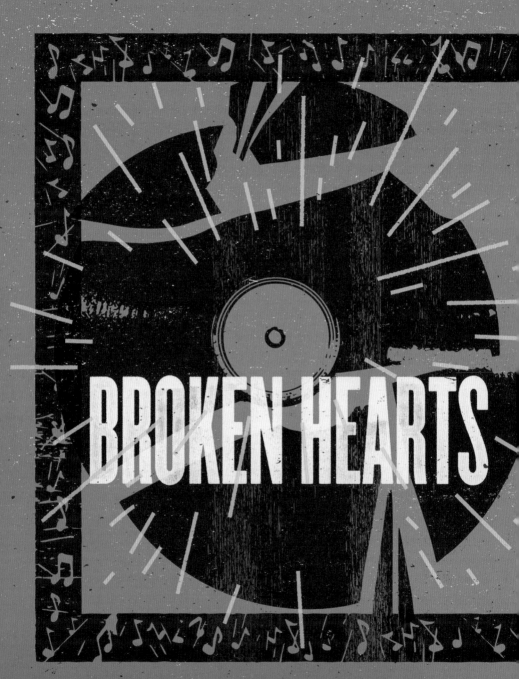

There are a lot of jokes about country music and heartbreak, but no other genre does it better. From cheating to divorce, distance to death, there's a song for every story of heartache. And country songs get right to the heart of heartbreak, dealing with not just the sadness, longing, and grief but also the vengeance, reinvention, and empowerment that often walk hand in hand.

When you're dealing with romance gone wrong, the songs in this section can make you rethink bad behavior, realize you're better off, or even just choose to be grateful for the time you had. From Patsy Cline's "She's Got You" to Taylor Swift's "Picture to Burn," country music has you covered. And for those whose loss cuts deeper, you've got songs that see your pain, like Carrie Underwood's "Just a Dream" and Lee Brice's "I Drive Your Truck." No matter what you're going through, country music is here to help you to the other side.

"LITTLE THINGS
I SHOULD HAVE
SAID AND DONE
I JUST NEVER
TOOK THE TIME"

ALWAYS ON MY MIND

Performed by Willie Nelson

WILLIE NELSON RELEASED HIS RENDITION OF "ALWAYS ON MY MIND"—the first to top the charts—in 1982, but the song's story is timeless. Most country fans know it well: the pain of regret, of wishing you had done more. The simplest gestures matter. They help you fall in love, and ignoring them can help your partner fall right out. A kind word, a thoughtful gift or act, or a warm embrace now and again lets someone know they're on your mind, and that can spare you both some heartbreak.

BEHIND THE MUSIC ▶ *Written by songwriter Wayne Carson (with a little help from Johnny Christopher and Mark James on the bridge), "Always on My Mind" is one of those songs that has stood the test of time and music history. Wayne told the Los Angeles Times that he wrote the bulk of it after apologizing to his wife, who was angry with him for staying in Memphis longer than he'd planned. He assured her he was always thinking of her, and the relatability of the sentiment hit him. The music world clearly felt it, too, because the song has been recorded by dozens of artists besides Willie, including Brenda Lee and Elvis Presley.*

THE DANCE

Performed by Garth Brooks

THE BEAUTY OF "THE DANCE" MAY BE IN THE EYE OF THE BEHOLDER. Like many listeners, songwriter Tony Arata saw the song as a lesson in appreciating the love you had even after it's gone. But Garth Brooks saw a deeper kind of hope and heartbreak in its lyrics. He filled the video with visions of Martin Luther King Jr., John F. Kennedy, and others whose dreams outlived them. The song has become as much a memorial to them as it is a message of love. It reminds fans that the pain of loss has its place in love and in life, and it doesn't erase all the good that came before it.

BEHIND THE MUSIC ▶ *One of the most moving songs in all of country music, "The Dance" is a timeless hit that almost wasn't. According to music publisher Dan Tolle, it was so different from anything being cut at the time that no label would touch it. But the song stuck with a young Garth Brooks, who heard it while hanging out at the famous Bluebird Café in Nashville. When he was later signed to a major label, Garth reached out to Tony for permission to record the song.*

"HEY,
WHO'S TO SAY,
YOU KNOW I MIGHT
HAVE CHANGED IT ALL"

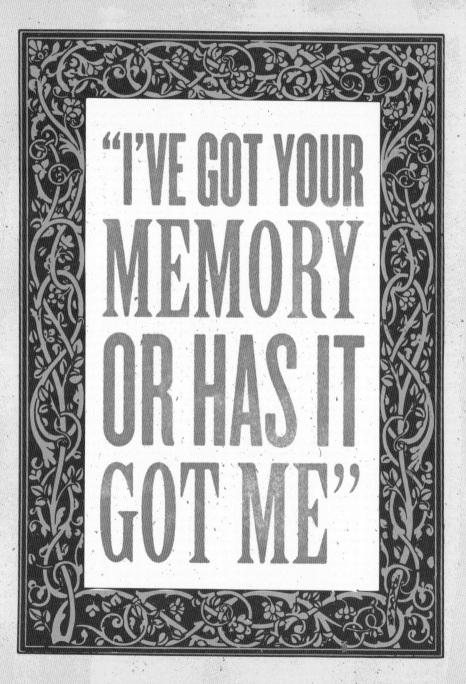

SHE'S GOT YOU

Performed by Patsy Cline

FEW COUNTRY MUSICIANS CAN SING ABOUT HEARTBREAK THE WAY PATSY CLINE DID. In "She's Got You," Patsy breathes emotion and life into the all-too-relatable story of someone who isn't ready to let go of their love. It's still there, coloring every memory and item left behind. This song is a hard lesson in moving on when there's nothing left to say. You can still cherish those little things, like a favorite song or a loving note, but you can't let them have power over you for too long.

BEHIND THE MUSIC ▶ *Songwriter Hank Cochran called up Patsy Cline the minute he'd finished writing "She's Got You" and told her he'd just written her next number-one hit. According to Hank, Patsy told him to come on over—liquor in hand—and play it for her and her friend, fellow country icon Dottie West. Patsy loved the song so much that she learned it that night and included it on her next studio album,* Sentimentally Yours.

PICTURE TO BURN

Performed by Taylor Swift

NO ONE DOES A BREAKUP SONG LIKE TAYLOR SWIFT, who pours her whole heart into the lyrics she writes. Although she doesn't shy away from more poignant stories, "Picture to Burn" is more like a pep talk for anyone who's wasted time on someone who wasn't worth it. And that's an awfully big percentage of the population. When someone like that breaks your heart, take a page out of Taylor's book: Strike a match and use it to look on the bright side. You're probably better off.

BEHIND THE MUSIC ▶ *Taylor has certainly moved on to bigger and better things since those early days, when she'd head into downtown Nashville after school to write songs for Sony. She's won dozens of awards for her music, including eleven Grammys and six American Music Awards for Artist of the Year—the most of any musician. And goodness knows she's not finished yet! The happiness and success she's created for herself are the ultimate revenge.*

"THE TIME WILL COME WHEN ⊿ YOU'LL BE BLUE"

YOUR CHEATIN' HEART

Performed by Hank Williams Sr.

NOT EVERY BROKEN HEART BELONGS TO THE ONE WHO'S BEEN WRONGED. In "Your Cheatin' Heart," Hank Williams sings about the sorrow and remorse that follow when you choose to cheat and hurt the one you love. If you go down that road, you had better be prepared to lose your love. They'll be right to walk away, and no amount of crying and pacing will bring them back once you realize you miss the love you threw away.

BEHIND THE MUSIC ▶ *Hank was rumored to have written the song about his ex-wife, Audrey, who left him after years of his substance abuse and infidelity. Ironically, he told his soon-to-be second wife, Billie Jean Jones, that Audrey was the one with a "cheatin' heart." The turn of phrase immediately inspired him to write the song, which Billie Jean took down on a notepad as he dictated it to her. Hank was married to Billie Jean for only a few months before he died of a heart attack, leaving Audrey to wonder whether she could have saved him from himself if only she had stayed.*

JUST A DREAM

Performed by Carrie Underwood

COUNTRY MUSIC HAS NEVER SHIED AWAY FROM TRAGEDY AND HEARTACHE. It helps you face them, giving you the words to express even the deepest pain. "Just a Dream" is one of those songs that dives right in and helps you come out on the other side with a story about the ultimate romantic heartbreak—the death of a partner. Carrie Underwood masterfully infuses the lyrics with the sense of denial, anger, and despair that follows a loss like that. When she sings "this can't be happening," she's singing for everyone who's felt that grief. Only by letting it out can you even begin to process it, and songs like this one help you do just that.

BEHIND THE MUSIC ▶ *Both the lyrics and the video depict songwriter Hillary Lindsey's vision: a young woman who goes from heading to the altar to marry the love of her life to standing over his casket. Hillary crafted the story with cowriters Gordie Sampson and Steve McEwan before handing it off to one of the few artists skilled enough to do it justice.*

"IT'S LIKE I'M LOOKING FROM A DISTANCE STANDING IN THE BACKGROUND"

"HE STILL LOVED HER
THROUGH IT ALL

HOPING SHE'D
COME BACK AGAIN"

HE STOPPED LOVING HER TODAY

Performed by George Jones

THEY SAY TIME HEALS ALL WOUNDS, but some broken hearts are just too stubborn to mend. That's especially true when it comes to the one who got away. The man in "He Stopped Loving Her Today" was stuck dwelling on a relationship that had long since expired. Because of that, he was gone before he even passed away. That's a lesson both in the powerful hold love can have on a person and in living while you're alive. Don't waste your life on long-lost love. Otherwise, they may as well carry you away today.

BEHIND THE MUSIC ▶ *Incredibly, it was this sad, slow song about death written by Bobby Braddock and Curly Putman that brought George Jones's career back to life. In his autobiography,* I Lived to Tell It All, *the singer admits he thought the song would be a flop. He stumbled through the lyrics, forcing producer Billy Sherrill to piece together multiple takes to get the finished recording. In the end, "He Stopped Loving Her Today" earned him multiple major awards and became known as one of the greatest country songs of all time.*

MISS ME MORE

Performed by Kelsea Ballerini

ONE OF THE GREAT THINGS ABOUT COUNTRY MUSIC is that you'll find as many empowering songs to choose from as you will sorrowful ones. When you're hemming and hawing about ending things, thinking about how much it'll hurt, Kelsea's here to remind you of how much you owe yourself. Giving yourself permission to break out your bright red lipstick and highest heels is just the beginning.

BEHIND THE MUSIC ▶ *The video, which was Kelsea's concept, shows her sparring against herself in the boxing ring. But backstage at the CMT Music Awards rehearsal, she clarified that the song isn't about fighting against anyone: "It's really about fighting for yourself. I just think it's a really important message, not just for girls, but for everyone to realize you're worth fighting for." Like filming the highly physical video was for Kelsea, fighting for what you want may be challenging. But post-breakup hits like "Miss Me More" will have you back to your fighting weight in no time.*

"I FOUND MY INDEPENDENCE CAN'T BELIEVE I EVER LOST IT"

"I'VE CUSSED,
I'VE PRAYED,
I'VE SAID
GOODBYE
SHOOK MY FIST
~AND~
ASKED GOD WHY"

I DRIVE YOUR TRUCK

Performed by Lee Brice

WHEN YOU THINK ABOUT BROKEN HEARTS, you might just think about romance gone wrong. But life has plenty of ways to break your heart, and losing a loved one or family member tops the list. Songs like Carrie Underwood's "Just a Dream" and Lee Brice's "I Drive Your Truck" make you feel like you're not alone in your grief. You can let the words wash over you, sing along at the top of your lungs, take your anger out on the steering wheel—everyone's got their own way of coping. But finding a way to feel close to the person you've lost is a good start.

BEHIND THE MUSIC ▶ *Tears welled up in songwriter Connie Harrington's eyes as she told Bart Herbison about the inspiration for the song: an NPR interview with Paul Monti, who had lost his son—Medal of Honor recipient Jared Monti—in Afghanistan. Paul said he coped with the pain by driving his son's truck. Together with Jessi Alexander and Jimmy Yeary, Connie wrote a song to honor his story of love and loss. In the process, she gave listeners an outlet for their own grief.*

TURN ON THE RADIO

Performed by Reba McEntire

WHEN REBA SINGS, YOU NEED TO TAKE NOTES. This queen of country music is well known for heartfelt ballads and chart-topping duets. But it's her joy and strength that shine through all of her music. "Turn on the Radio" is no exception, turning the "done me wrong" song on its ear by telling her cheating ex where he can go. While he's tied up with regrets (and microphone cord, in the video), she's on to bigger and better things. That's the attitude you want to bring to every breakup.

BEHIND THE MUSIC ▶ *When Cherie Oakley first wrote "Turn on the Radio" with Mark Oakley and J. P. Twang, she had no idea someone like Reba would come along to record it. But the country icon herself called Cherie up to request permission to cut the song just a few days after the trio had written it. Cherie recalled in an interview for* The Boot *that Reba was thrilled when she said yes, saying, "You have made my day, Cherie." But Cherie said it was the other way around, and she was blown away by how the song turned out.*

"BROKE MY HEART, TORE IT APART, LOOK WHO'S GOT THE LAST LAUGH NOW"

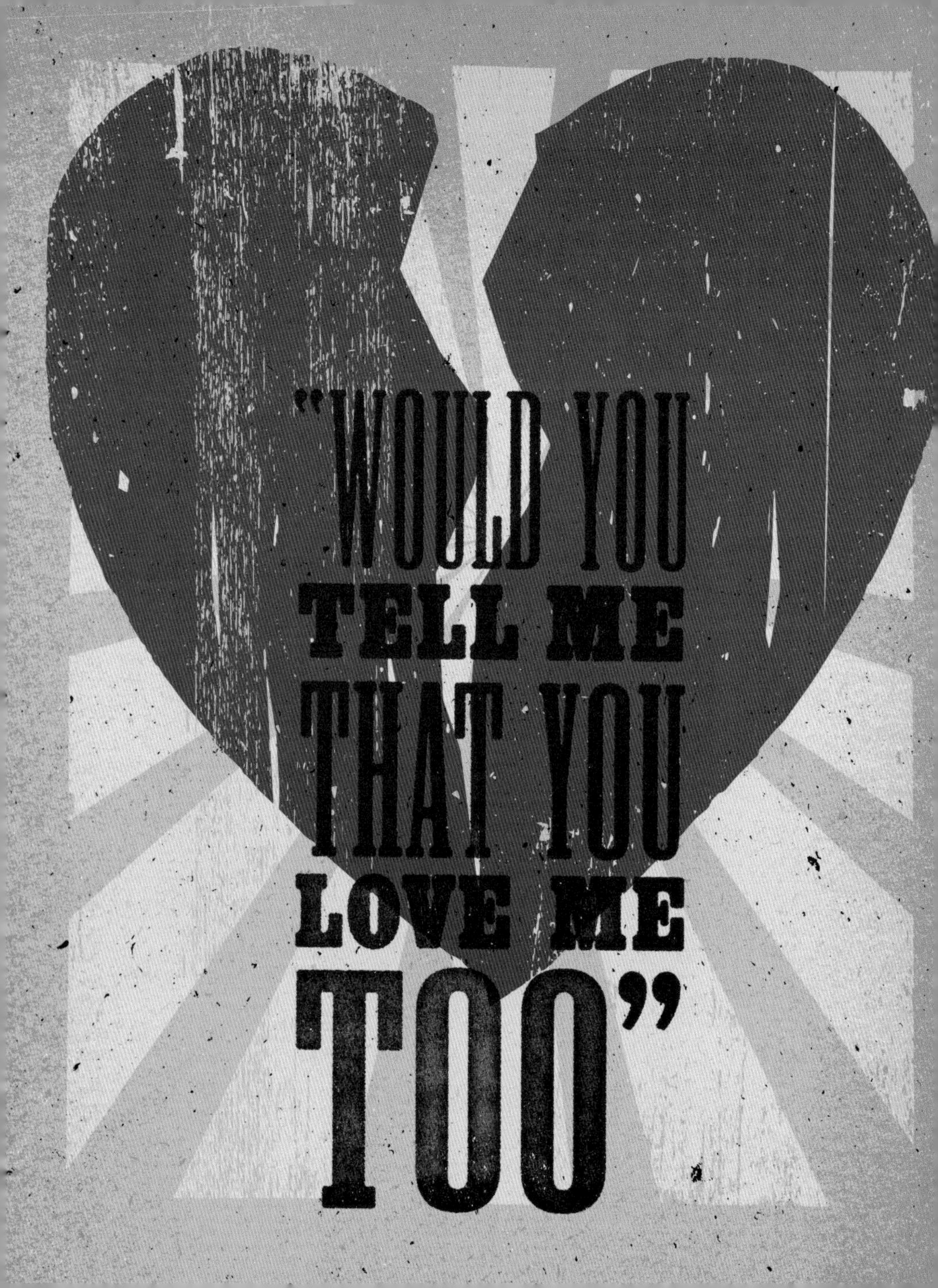
"WOULD YOU
TELL ME
THAT YOU
LOVE ME
TOO"

I TOLD YOU SO

Performed by Randy Travis

SECOND CHANCES ARE PART OF LIFE, so you'll find plenty of them in country music. You just won't find any in "I Told You So." Instead, Randy Travis offers you a hard-won lesson: that you can't always walk back your mistakes. When you leave someone, you had better be sure it's what you really want. Odds are, by the time you come crawling back, they'll have found somebody new. And the only thing that will be yours forever is your regret.

BEHIND THE MUSIC ▶ *The song itself got a second chance in 2007, and Randy couldn't be happier with how things turned out. Carrie Underwood covered "I Told You So" for her sophomore album, Carnival Ride, breathing new life into the lyrics. The pair then released a duet version of the song, which earned them a Grammy in 2010 for Best Country Collaboration with Vocals. Randy suddenly found his song climbing the charts more than twenty years after its first release. To top it all off, he had the honor of surprising Carrie with an invitation to join the Grand Ole Opry just after she'd performed the song there.*

You can find some of the best life advice in country songs because that's what country music is. It's all just stories about life: living it, loving it, and learning from it. Country artists have some pretty big dreams, so you'll find plenty of songs about going after what you want. But there's also a humility and grace to the music. Country artists remember where they came from, put a premium on gratitude and warmth, and know when to let their faith take the wheel.

The songs in this section offer just a small sample of the many words of wisdom you can find in country music. But it's a good sample. With death-defying advice from Tim McGraw you can't hear too often, a little encouragement from Miranda Lambert and Gary Allan to help you weather life's storms, and a much-needed reminder from Luke Bryan that most people are good, these songs might just give you a new lease on life.

"IF YOU GOT A DREAM, CHASE IT"

'TIL YOU CAN'T

Performed by Cody Johnson

WHEN THE KIDS ARE YELLING, THE DOG NEEDS FEEDING, AND THE BOSS IS ON YOU, it's all too easy to get caught up in the busyness of everyday life. But tomorrow isn't promised to any of us. "'Til You Can't" is a great reminder of what we stand to lose when we take life for granted, and how much we have to gain by seizing every moment. So spend time with the people you love, chase that dream, and make the most of every day you're given.

BEHIND THE MUSIC ▶ *Cody Johnson himself learned the song's lesson the hard way. In 2021, he was on a small private plane with his wife and management team when the pilot said, "You need to prepare yourself. We're going down." He told* Taste of Country Nights *that the plane dropped from 39,000 feet to 15,000 feet while alarms rang out and panels fell off the walls. Thankfully, the pilot was able to land the plane safely. But Cody says the experience helped him appreciate the song (which was written by Ben Stennis and Matt Rogers) and his time on Earth more than ever.*

CHICKEN FRIED

Performed by Zac Brown Band

"CHICKEN FRIED" IS ONE OF THOSE UPBEAT, FEEL-GOOD SONGS that has made every country fan's playlist over the years. But there's more to it than you might think. Working on the song just after September 11, Zac started to see life's simple pleasures a little differently. He realized how fortunate he was, as an American, to enjoy them, and that his good fortune was because of brave men and women who sacrificed everything. Zac wants "Chicken Fried" to serve as a reminder never to take those things for granted. The best things in life might be simple, but they aren't free.

BEHIND THE MUSIC ▶ *Zac told* The Boot *that he and cowriter Wyatt Durrette tried to squeeze into the song all the things that mattered to them and to the south. When it came down to it, they were all simple, everyday things like cold beer, a mother's love, the sunrise, and fried chicken. "Sometimes all of the little things get taken for granted, and you forget about them," Zac said. "They're the most important things in life."*

"IT'S FUNNY
HOW IT'S THE
LITTLE THINGS IN LIFE
THAT MEAN
THE MOST"

"THERE'S BEEN A LOAD OF COMPROMISIN'

ON THE ROAD TO MY HORIZON"

RHINESTONE COWBOY

Performed by Glen Campbell

YOU DON'T GET ANYWHERE IN LIFE WITHOUT HARD WORK AND SACRIFICE, but your dreams are sometimes the only things that will keep you going. When Glen Campbell first heard that lesson in the lyrics of Larry Weiss's "Rhinestone Cowboy," he could identify. Sure, he had his own television show. But he was going through a divorce, struggling with substance abuse, and hadn't had a hit in years. Like the protagonist in the song, Glen kept his eye on the bright horizon rather than on the rain pouring down on him, and it paid off. His story proves it's not a bad idea to put your focus on the good things to come.

BEHIND THE MUSIC ▶ *According to Larry's interview with The Guardian, Glen said he was so struck by the song when he first heard it played on the radio that he had to pull his car over. He knew he'd found something special. Before Glen came looking to record the song, Larry had been ready to give up on it. "The song had been turned down by everybody from Elvis Presley to Neil Diamond," he said. But with Glen singing it, "Rhinestone Cowboy" topped the charts in both country and pop music.*

BLUEBIRD

Performed by Miranda Lambert

IF THERE'S ANYONE WHO KNOWS HOW TO ROLL WITH THE PUNCHES, it's Miranda Lambert. Some of her songs punch back, some suggest turning the other cheek. But "Bluebird" beats them all when it comes to good advice. The bottom line? The only thing in this life you can control is you. When you're feeling beaten down or broken, you can make a change or walk away. But the best thing you can do is keep that inner light on by having faith in yourself and your ability to deal with whatever life throws at you.

BEHIND THE MUSIC ▶ *When it came time to write songs for* Wildcard, *cowriter Luke Dick told Miranda he wanted to write about keeping a bluebird in your heart because that's what she did, especially throughout her divorce from fellow country musician Blake Shelton. Along with Natalie Hemby, they created a song that Miranda said felt magical. "When I sing this song, I feel a little flutter," she said at an album preview event. "I feel every single word of what it means."*

"I BECAME A FRIEND A FRIEND WOULD LIKE TO HAVE"

LIVE LIKE YOU WERE DYING

Performed by Tim McGraw

IT'S NOT HARD TO FIGURE OUT THE LESSON IN THIS TIM MCGRAW HIT—it's right there in the title. The trick is to figure out what it means to you. If this were your last month on Earth, how would you spend it? That's the question songwriters Craig Wiseman and Tim Nichols asked themselves when they started to work on "Live Like You Were Dying." Before long, they had written a song that would sit at number one for seven weeks and win every major award in country music. The song resonated with fans because its story is all too common. So don't wait to make the most of the time you're given. All those things you said you'd do someday? Now's the time to start doing them.

BEHIND THE MUSIC ▶ *Tim McGraw said on his radio show,* Beyond the Influence, *that the song came at a traumatic time in his life. His father, former Major League Baseball player Tug McGraw, had died of brain cancer just weeks earlier. But Tim described recording the song with his father's brother in the studio as "one of the most special memories I have of making any music anywhere."*

THE GAMBLER

Performed by Kenny Rogers

As far as stories go, "The Gambler" might seem like a pretty straightforward one. But a lot of people miss the moral. The advice the old stranger imparts isn't just that you have to know when to throw in the towel. It's that every hand has the potential to go either way. What you choose to do with it makes the difference. In every situation, you have a choice: let go or hold on. Knowing *how* to choose is important, but knowing that you *have* a choice is the real lesson here.

BEHIND THE MUSIC ▶ *Kenny Rogers's "The Gambler" is so ingrained in music history that you might not even know that Bobby Bare, Johnny Cash, and the song's writer, Don Schlitz, all cut the song before him. None had his success with it. With Kenny on vocals, the song climbed to number one, won Grammys, and inspired a series of Emmy-winning television specials. According to an interview with* American Songwriter, *it also helped Don go from a nighttime computer programmer to a full-time songwriter responsible for such hits as Randy Travis's "Forever and Ever, Amen."*

"THE SECRET TO SURVIVIN' IS KNOWIN' WHAT TO THROW AWAY AND KNOWIN' WHAT TO KEEP"

"SO PICK YOUR FLOWERS,
— count the seconds, —
ROLL THE DICE"

THESE ARE THE DAYS

Performed by Jo Dee Messina

IF YOU BELIEVE THAT HAPPINESS IS JUST AROUND THE BEND, you could spend your whole life chasing it. But you can choose to be happy right now, in this and every moment, instead. Sure, your dreams might be taking their sweet time to come true, and the day-to-day stuff might be driving you crazy, but you only get one life. "These Are the Days" forces you to ask yourself what you want to remember about it: the rushing to get ahead, or the warmth of the sun on your face?

BEHIND THE MUSIC ▶ *The song may have been written by Holly Lamar and Stephanie Bentley, but Jo Dee Messina also falls squarely in the "savoring the sunshine" camp. She told* Songfacts *that "just [having] a chance to get to live through the day or see another day, that's a blessing, and I'm just really grateful." That gratitude and positivity, as well as an unwavering faith in God, has helped Jo Dee through some tough times in more recent years, including a battle with cancer. But she continues to choose happiness and hope every day.*

EVERY STORM (RUNS OUT OF RAIN)

Performed by Gary Allan

SEARCH FOR "EVERY STORM" ONLINE, AND YOU'LL FIND COUNTLESS STORIES about how this song has helped country music fans through their darkest nights. In his video, singing while soaked to the bone, Gary Allan reminds fans to stand strong through the tough times and remember that even the worst times are only temporary. It may not feel like it when you're surrounded by thunder and lightning, but the rain will stop and the sun will shine again. Keeping the faith isn't easy, but it's the best way to ride out the storm.

BEHIND THE MUSIC ▶ *Matt Warren already had the song's message in mind when he found himself in the middle of his own storm. Dropped by his publisher, Matt was living with a friend and working in landscaping to make ends meet. But he kept the faith. He brought the concept for "Every Storm" to his favorite cowriters, Hillary Lindsey and Gary Allan, who helped him turn it into a chart-topping single on Gary's album* Set You Free. *Today, Matt says he's "living [his] dream."*

"SO HOLD YOUR HEAD UP
AND TELL YOURSELF

THAT THERE'S
SOMETHING MORE"

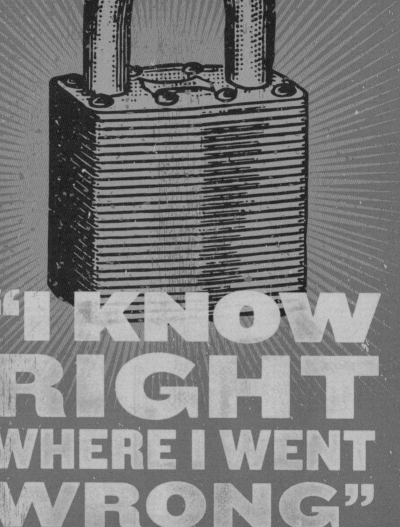

"I KNOW RIGHT WHERE I WENT WRONG"

NOBODY TO BLAME

Performed by Chris Stapleton

COUNTRY CROONERS ARE PRETTY GOOD AT ACCEPTING RESPONSIBILITY FOR THEIR ACTIONS, if only a little too late to save their relationships. Although you could see "Nobody to Blame" as just another country song about heartbreak, it's really a lesson in learning from your mistakes. If you take the time to see where you went wrong, you give yourself the power to stop it from happening again. And maybe next time, you'll be able to right the ship before your partner throws your clothes out in the yard.

BEHIND THE MUSIC ▶ *With hits like this one, you might think Chris Stapleton has always been a household name. But he had a long career writing for other music stars, like Kenny Chesney and George Strait, before getting his own big break. When he cowrote "Nobody to Blame" with Barry Bales and Ronnie Bowman, they were looking for someone else to cut it. Barry told The Boot, "I never dreamed it would be Chris cutting it and having success with it." But he was thrilled to see his talented friend finally take center stage.*

MOST PEOPLE ARE GOOD

Performed by Luke Bryan

COUNTRY MUSIC IS FULL OF OPINIONS ABOUT WHAT MATTERS MOST IN LIFE, and you can be sure it's never the material things. For songwriters Josh Kear, Ed Hill, and David Frazier, life is about the people. "Most People Are Good" is a much-needed reminder that everyone is out there just trying to do their best, same as you. So, love who you love, thank your mama, forgive old friends, spend your Friday nights surrounded by good people, and watch as the world gets better right before your eyes.

BEHIND THE MUSIC ▶ *Josh, Ed, and David wrote "Most People Are Good" in 2016, when the country was especially divided and, as Josh put it to interviewer Bart Herbison, "it kind of all felt icky." When he shared the idea for the song with his cowriters during one of their weekly writing sessions, they immediately agreed with its message. And so did Luke Bryan, who took the song to the number-one spot. It was a refreshing change of pace from the party songs playing across country radio at the time, and it instantly hit home with fans.*

"EVERY BREATH'S A GIFT THE FIRST ONE TO THE LAST"

YOUR PLAYLIST

DOWN HOME

- "You're Lookin' at Country," Loretta Lynn
- "Girl in a Country Song," Maddie & Tae
- "I Love This Bar," Toby Keith
- "May We All," Florida Georgia Line and Tim McGraw
- "Cowboy Take Me Away," The Chicks
- "Champagne Night," Lady A
- "Alright," Darius Rucker
- "Rocky Mountain High," John Denver
- "Merry Go 'Round," Kacey Musgraves
- "Raised on Country," Chris Young

GROWING UP

- "You're Gonna Miss This," Trace Adkins
- "Wild One," Faith Hill
- "Letter to Me," Brad Paisley
- "Invisible," Hunter Hayes
- "Sixteen," Thomas Rhett
- "Red Dirt Road," Brooks & Dunn
- "This One's for the Girls," Martina McBride
- "The Impossible," Joe Nichols
- "My Wish," Rascal Flatts
- "Remember When," Alan Jackson

GOOD TIMES

- "House Party," Sam Hunt
- "No Shoes, No Shirt, No Problems," Kenny Chesney
- "'80s Mercedes," Maren Morris
- "Talladega," Eric Church
- "Pontoon," Little Big Town
- "All About Tonight," Blake Shelton
- "What Was I Thinkin'," Dierks Bentley
- "Down in Mississippi (Up to No Good)," Sugarland
- "Barefoot Blue Jean Night," Jake Owen
- "Five More Minutes," Scotty McCreery

REAL LOVE

- "I Will Always Love You," Dolly Parton
- "You're My Better Half," Keith Urban
- "I Walk the Line," Johnny Cash
- "You're Still the One," Shania Twain
- "Speechless," Dan + Shay
- "Homesick," Kane Brown
- "Love Can Build a Bridge," The Judds
- "Check Yes or No," George Strait
- "Don't Let Our Love Start Slippin' Away," Vince Gill
- "Beautiful Crazy," Luke Combs
- "She's in Love with the Boy," Trisha Yearwood

BROKEN HEARTS

- "Always on My Mind," Willie Nelson
- "The Dance," Garth Brooks
- "She's Got You," Patsy Cline
- "Picture to Burn," Taylor Swift
- "Your Cheatin' Heart," Hank Williams Sr.
- "Just a Dream," Carrie Underwood
- "He Stopped Loving Her Today," George Jones
- "Miss Me More," Kelsea Ballerini
- "I Drive Your Truck," Lee Brice
- "Turn on the Radio," Reba McEntire
- "I Told You So," Randy Travis

LIVIN' LIFE

- "'Til You Can't," Cody Johnson
- "Chicken Fried," Zac Brown Band
- "Rhinestone Cowboy," Glen Campbell
- "Bluebird," Miranda Lambert
- "Live Like You Were Dying," Tim McGraw
- "The Gambler," Kenny Rogers
- "These Are the Days," Jo Dee Messina
- "Every Storm (Runs Out of Rain)," Gary Allan
- "Nobody to Blame," Chris Stapleton
- "Most People Are Good," Luke Bryan